Rudolf   Steiner

The Education of Children

From the standpoint of Theosophy

Rudolf   Steiner

The Education of Children
From the standpoint of Theosophy

ISBN/EAN: 9783337364878

Printed in Europe, USA, Canada, Australia, Japan

Cover: Foto ©Paul-Georg Meister /pixelio.de

More available books at **www.hansebooks.com**

THE EDUCATION
OF CHILDREN

FROM THE STANDPOINT
OF THEOSOPHY

BY

RUDOLF STEINER
PH. D. (VIENNA)

AUTHORIZED TRANSLATION
FROM THE SECOND GERMAN EDITION

AMERICAN EDITION

THE RAJPUT PRESS.

CHICAGO.
1911

MAX GYSI, Editor,
"Adyar," Park Drive,
Hampstead, London, N. W.

THE
EDUCATION OF CHILDREN

FROM THE STANDPOINT OF THEOSOPHY

(TRANSLATED BY W. B.)

Present day life calls into question many things which man has inherited from his ancestors hence the numberless questions of the day, as for example: the Social Problem, the Woman's Movement, Education and School Questions, Law Reform, Hygiene, Sanitation, and so forth. We try to grapple with these questions in manifold ways. The number of those who bring forward this or that remedy in order to solve this or that question, or at least to contribute something towards its solution, is immeasurably great, and every possible shade of opinion is manifested in these endeavors; radicalism, carrying itself with a revolutionary air; the moderate view, full of respect for existing things and desirous of fashioning out of them something new; or conservatism, up in arms, whenever old institutions and traditions are tampered with; and besides these main attitudes, there are all sorts of intermediary points of view.

He who is able to probe deeply into life cannot help feeling one thing with regard to these phenomena—that the claims which are placed before men in our time are met repeatedly by inadequate means. Many would like to re-form life, without really knowing it from its foundations. He who would put forth a proposition as to life in the future, must not content himself with merely learning to know life superficially. He must probe it to its depths.

Life is like a plant that contains not only that which is visible to the eye, but also a future condition concealed within its secret depths. He who has before him a plant that

5

is just in leaf, is well aware that later on blossoms and fruit will be added to the leaf-bearing stem. The germs of these blossoms and fruit are already concealed within the plant. But it is impossible for one who merely regards it in its present condition to say how these organs will ultimately appear. Only he who is acquainted with the nature of the plant can do so.

Human life also contains within itself the germs for its future. But to be able to say anything about this future one must penetrate into the hidden nature of man, and this, the present age, has no real inclination to do. It busies itself with the surface and thinks itself treading on unsafe ground should it advance into that which is hidden from external observation. With the plant it is true the matter is considerably simpler. We know that its like has often and often brought forth flowers and fruit. Human life exists but once and the flowers which it is to bring forth in the future were not previously there. None the less they exist in human life in embryo, just as much as the flowers of the plant which at present is only just bearing leaves.

And it is possible to say something about this future, when one penetrates beneath the surface, into the heart of human nature. The different reformatory ideas of the present can only become really fruitful and practical, when they are the result of this deep research into human life.

Theosophy is suited by its very nature to present a practical philosophy, comprehending the whole sphere of human life. Whether or not Theosophy, or that which in our time so often passes for it, is justified in putting forth such a claim, is not the point. The point concerns rather the nature of Theosophy and what, by means of this nature, it is able to accomplish. It ought not to be a colorless theory to satisfy the mere curiosity of knowledge, nor yet a medium for those men who, out of selfishness, would like to win for themselves a higher grade of evolution. It can contribute something to the most important problems of present day Humanity, in the development of its well-being.

Of course if it acknowledges a mission of this kind it must expect to meet with all manner of opposition and doubt. Radicals, Moderates and Conservatives of all departments in life will surely raise such doubts against it. For at first it will be unable to please any one party, because its doctrines reach far beyond all party motives.

And these doctrines have their roots wholly and solely in the true understanding of life. Only he who understands life will be able to take his lessons from life itself. He will draw up no capricious schemes, for he knows that no other fundamental laws of life will prevail in the future than such as prevail in the present. Theosophy will therefore of necessity have respect for the existing state of things. Even, should it still find in what is existent, very much that might be improved, yet it will not fail to perceive in the present the germs of the future. But it knows, too, that for all things nascent there is a growth and a development. Therefore the germs for a transformation and for a future growth will appear to Theosophy in the existing state of things. It invents no schemes, it only calls them forth from what already exists. But that which is so called forth becomes in a certain sense itself a scheme, for it contains within itself the nature of evolution.

For this very reason the theosophical way of delving into the nature of man must yield the most fruitful and practical means for the solution of the vitally important questions of the present time.

It is my purpose to apply this to one such question, namely that of education. We do not intend to advance any claims or pronounce a learned dissertation, but to portray simply the child nature. From a study of the nature of the growing man, the educational standpoint here suggested will develop quite naturally. But to proceed rightly with such a study it is necessary to contemplate the hidden nature of man in general.

That which is cognised by the physical perception, that which the materialistic view of life considers to be the only important element in the nature of man, namely, his physical body, forms, according to spiritual research, only a part, a principle of human nature. This physical body is subject to the same laws of physical life, is composed of the same matter and forces, as all the rest of the so-called lifeless world. Theosophy, therefore, maintains that man possesses this physical aspect in common with the whole of the mineral kingdom. And it considers as physical body that part only in man which is able to mix, unite, to build up and to dissolve the very same materials, and after identical laws, as are also at work in the mineral world.

Now besides this physical body, Theosophy recognizes a second element in the constitution of man—namely a vital or etheric body. And that there may be no cause for the physicist to reject the term etheric body we would point out that etheric is here used in a different sense from the hypothetical ether of physics, and it must be taken to mean here that which is about to be described.

It has been considered for some time past a most unscientific proceeding to speak of an "etheric body" of this kind. At the end of the eighteenth and in the first half of the nineteenth century, it is true, it was not considered "unscientific." It was then said that matter and force operating in a mineral could not of their own power form themselves into a living being. For this there must be an especial indwelling "force," which was termed "vital force." It was represented indeed that such a force operates in plants, in animals, and in human bodies, and produces the phenomena of life just as magnetic force in the magnet causes attraction. In the succeeding period of materialism this theory had been abandoned. It was then said that a living being builds itself up in the same way as a so-called lifeless being; no other forces prevail in an organism than those which are in the mineral—they only operate in a more complicated manner; they build up a more complex structure. At the present time, only the most obstinate materialists cling to this denial of the "vital force." A number of natural philosophers have taught that one must nevertheless admit some such thing as a vital force of a life-principle.

Thus the new science approaches in a certain sense the teaching of Theosophy in regard to the vital body. Nevertheless there is a considerable difference between the two. Science today, by means of intellectual observations founded on the facts of ordinary perception, has accepted the idea of a kind of vital force. But this is not the method of a truly spiritual research, such as Theosophy aims at, and from the results of which proceed the theosophical teachings. It cannot be pointed out too often, how Theosophy on this point differs from the current science of the day. The latter considers the experience of the senses to be the basis of all knowledge, and whatever is not built upon this basis it treats as unknowable. From the impressions of the senses it draws deductions and conclusions. But anything that goes further it puts aside, as being beyond the limits of human knowledge. To Theosophy such a prospect resembles the view of a blind man who only takes into consideration those things that he can touch, and what he may infer from the touched object by reasoning, but who sets aside the statements of those

9

who can see as being beyond the faculty of human perception. For Theosophy shows that man is capable of evolution, that through the developing of new organs he may conquer for himself new worlds. Around the blind man there is color and light, but he cannot perceive them, because he does not possess the requisite organs. Around man, so Theosophy teaches, there are many worlds, and he can observe them, if only he develops the organs necessary for the purpose.

Even as the blind man looks upon a new world as soon as he has undergone a successful operation, so can man, through the developing of higher organs, perceive worlds quite different from those which he observed at first with his ordinary senses. Now whether or not it is possible to operate on one who is bodily blind depends on the conditions of the organs; but those higher organs by which one may penetrate into the upper worlds, exist in embryo in every human being. Anyone can develop them, who has the patience, endurance and energy to make use of those methods which are described in my two books entitled "The Way of Initiation" and "Initiation and Its Results."[1]

Theosophy does not speak of limitations to man's knowledge through his organism; but says, on the contrary, that he is surrounded by worlds for which he has the organs of perception. It indicates the means by which to extend the temporary limits. It also occupies itself with the investigation of the vital, or etheric body, and to what in the following may be called the yet higher principles of human nature. It admits that only the physical body can be accessible to the investigation of the bodily senses, and that from this standpoint one can at most only chance on something higher by a train of reasoning. But it gives information as to how one can open up for oneself a world in which these higher principles of human nature appear

10

before the observer, just as the colors and light of objects appear before the blind-born person after his operation. For those who have developed the higher organs of perception, the etheric or vital body is an object of actual observation, and not a theory resulting from intellectual activity or a train of reasoning.

Man has this etheric, or vital body, in common with the plants and animals. It causes the matter and forces of the physical body to form themselves into the manifestations of growth, of reproduction, of the internal motions of the fluids, etc. It is also the builder and sculptor of the physical body, its inhabitant and its architect. The physical body can therefore also be called an image or expression of this vital body. Both are approximately the same in man as regards form and size, yet they are by no means quite alike. But the etheric body in animals and still more in plants, differs considerably from the physical body with regard to its shape and dimension.

The third principle of the human being is the so-called body of feeling, or astral body. It is the vehicle of pain and pleasure, of impulse, desire, passion, and so forth. An entity composed merely of a physical and an etheric body has nothing of all this, to which may be ascribed the term— sensation. The plant has no sensation. If many a learned man of our time concludes that plants have a certain power of sensation, from the fact that many of them respond to a stimulus, by movement, or in other ways, he merely shows that he does not know the essence of sensation. The point is, not whether the being in question responds to an outward stimulus, but rather whether the stimulus reflects itself through an inner experience, such as pleasure or pain, impulse, desire, etc. If this be not the standard of sensation, one would be justified in asserting that blue litmus paper has a sense of feeling for certain substances, because on coming into contact with them, it turns red.[2]

Man has the astral body in common with the animal world only. It is thus the medium for the life of sensation and feeling.

One must not fall into the error of certain theosophical circles and think that the etheric body and

astral body consist merely of finer matter than that which exists in the physical body. For this would mean simply the materialisation of these higher principles of human nature. The etheric body is a form of living forces; it is composed of active forces, but not of matter — and the astral body or body of feeling is a form consisting of colored luminous pictures revolving within themselves.[3]

The astral body differs in form and size from the physical body. It appears in man in the form of an oblong egg, in which the physical and the etheric bodies are embedded. It projects on all sides beyond these two like a luminous cloud.

Now in the nature of man there is a fourth principle which he does not share with other earthly creatures. This is the vehicle of the human "I". The little word "I" as we call it in English is a word that separates itself from all other words. He who duly reflects on

the nature of this word, gains access at the same time to an understanding of human nature. Every other word may be used by all men in the same way to suit some corresponding object. Anyone can call a table "table," any one can call a chair "chair," but with the word "I" it is not so. No one can use it as an indication of some one else, for each person can only speak of himself as "I". Never can the word "I" sound in my ears as a reference to myself. For a man in designating himself "I", must name himself within himself. A being that can say to himself "I" is a world in himself. Those religions which are built up on the basis of Theosophy have always felt this. They have therefore said that with the "ego" the God begins to speak within—the God who, among lower beings, is manifested only from without in the surrounding phenomena.

The vehicle of this lastly developed capacity is now "the body of the ego," the fourth principle of the human being.[4] This body of the ego is the vehicle of the higher human soul, and through it man is the crown of all earthly creation. But the ego in present humanity is by no means a simple entity. Its nature can be recognized when a comparison is made between men of different stages of evolution. Take for instance the uneducated savage and the average European, and compare these again with a lofty idealist. Each one of them has the faculty of saying to himself "I" for the "body of the ego" is existent in each of them. But the uncivilized savage gives way with this "I" to his passions, his impulses and appetites, almost like an animal. The more highly developed man allows himself to follow certain inclinations and desires, others he checks or suppresses. The idealist has formed, in addition to the original inclinations and passions, others that are higher. This is all due to the fact that the "ego" has been at work on the other principles of the human being. And it is precisely the mission of the "ego" to ennoble and purify the other principles by its own power.

So the lower principles, under the influence of the "ego," have become more or less changed within a man who has surmounted the conditions in which the outer world has placed him. Take the case of the man who is just raising himself above the level of the animal—when his "ego" flashes out he still resembles the animal with regard to his lower principles. His etheric or vital body is solely the

13

medium of the living constructive forces of growth and propagation. His astral body only gives expression to such impulses, desires and passions as are stimulated by his outer nature. All the time that the man is struggling on through successive lives, or incarnations, from this degree of culture to an ever higher evolution, his ego is remodelling the other principles. In this way the astral body becomes the medium of purified pleasurable and unpleasurable sensations, refined desires and longings. And the etheric, or vital body, also transforms itself. It becomes the vehicle of habits, of permanent inclinations of temperament and of memory. A man whose ego has not yet influenced his vital body has no remembrance of the experiences he undergoes. He lives just as he has been brought up by Nature.

The whole development of civilisation expresses itself for man in this working of the ego upon the subordinate principles. This working penetrates even to the physical body. Under the influence of the ego, the physiognomy, the gestures and movements, the whole appearance of the physical body, change.

One can also discern how differently the various mediums of civilisation affect the individual principles of the human being. The common factors of civilisation influence the astral body. They bring to it other kinds of pleasure, displeasure, impulse, etc., than it originally had. Absorption in a work of art influences the etheric body, for a man obtains through a work of art, the presentiment of something higher and nobler than that which is offered by the environment of the senses, and thus transforms his vital body. A powerful means for the purification and ennoblement of the etheric body is religion. Religious impulses have, in this way, their sublime mission in the evolution of humanity.

That which is called conscience is nothing but the result of the work of the ego on the vital body, through a succession of incarnations. When a man perceives that he must not do certain things, and when through this perception, an impression is made on him, deep enough to communicate itself to his etheric body, the conscience begins to be formed.

Now this work of the ego on the subordinate principles can either be one that belongs rather to the whole human race, or it can be quite individually a work of the single ego upon itself. In the first change of man, to a certain extent, the whole human race takes part; the latter must depend on the inner activity of the ego. When the ego grows strong enough entirely to remodel the astral body through its own strength, then that which the ego makes of this astral body or body of feeling is called the "Spirit-Self" (Geistesselbst)[5] or as they say in the East, Manas. This transformation consists essentially in an imbuing, in an enriching of the inner being with higher ideas and perceptions. But the ego can arrive at yet higher and more intimate work with regard to the special entity of man. This occurs when not merely the astral body is enriched, but when the etheric or vital body becomes transformed. Man learns a certain amount in the course of life, and when he looks back on his life from any point, he is able to say to himself: "I have learnt much," but how much less is he able to speak of a change of temperament and character, of an improvement or deterioration of the memory, during life. Learning affects the astral body, whilst the latter transformations affect the ethic or vital body. It would therefore be no inapt simile to compare the change of the astral body in life to the movement of the minute-hand of the clock, the change of the vital body to that of the hour-hand.

When a man enters upon the higher, or so-called occult training, the chief thing to bear in mind is that he at once

15

begins this latter transformation by the innermost might of the ego. He must work quite consciously and individually at the changing of habits, temperament, character, memory, etc. As much of this vital body as he works upon in this way becomes transformed into the "Life-Spirit" (Lebensgeist), or as the Eastern expression has it, into Buddhi.

On a yet higher stage of evolution man attains to powers by which he can effect a transformation of his physical body (as for example, changing the pulse and the circulation of the blood). As much of the physical body as is transformed in this way, is called "Spirit-Man" (Geistesmensch)—Atma.

The changes which are effected in the lower principles by man, not as an individual, but rather as a whole group of the human race, or a part of it, such as a nation, a tribe, or a family—have in Theosophy, the following names. The astral body, or body of feeling, when transformed by the ego is called the emotional soul; the transformed etheric body becomes the rational soul, and the transformed physical body, the self-conscious soul. But it is not to be supposed that the transformation of these three principles takes place successively. It takes place in all three bodies simultaneously, from the moment when the ego flashes out. Indeed the work of the ego is not generally speaking perceptible until a part of the self-conscious soul is formed.

It is seen from the foregoing paragraph that there are four principles in the Being of Man: the physical body, the etheric or vital body, the astral or body of feeling and the ego-body; —the emotional soul, the rational soul, the self-conscious soul—and indeed the yet higher principles of human nature also,—the Spirit-Self (Manas), the Life-Spirit (Buddhi), the Spirit-Man (Atma) appear as the products of the transformation of these four principles. In speaking about the sources of our human capacities, only these four principles can be taken into account.

As a teacher works upon these four principles of the human constitution, one must, in order to work in the right way, penetrate into the nature of these divisions of man. Now it must by no means be imagined that these parts develop themselves in man in such a way that at any one moment of his life—say at his birth—they are all equally advanced. On the contrary their development takes place at the various life-periods in a different way. And the right foundations for education and instruction depend on the knowledge of this law of the evolution of human nature.

Before physical birth the nascent human being is enclosed on all sides by an alien physical body. It does not come into contact independently with the outward physical world. The physical body of the mother forms its environment. This body alone can influence the maturing fœtus. Physical birth consists precisely in the fact that the physical body of the mother releases the child, thereby causing the surroundings of the physical world to influence him immediately. The senses open themselves to the outward world, and this latter is thereby able to exercise those influences over the child which were previously exercised by the physical body of the mother.

For a spiritual comprehension of the world such as is represented by Theosophy, the physical body is then actually born, but not yet the etheric or vital body. As the child until the moment of its birth is surrounded by the physical body of the mother, so too until the time of his second teeth, about the age of seven, is he surrounded by an etheric and an astral covering. Not until the time of the change of teeth does the etheric covering release the etheric body. Then until the time of puberty there still remains an

17

astral covering.[6] At this period the astral or desire body also becomes free on all sides, as did the physical body at the time of the physical birth and the etheric body at the time of the second teeth.

Thus then, Theosophy must speak of three births of man. Certain impressions, which are intended to reach the etheric body can reach it as little, up to the time of the second teeth, as the light and air of the physical world can reach the physical body while it remains in the womb of the mother.

Before the coming of the second teeth the free vital body is not at work. As the physical body, whilst in the womb of the mother, receives powers which are not its own, and within that protective covering gradually develops its own, so is this also the case with these later powers of growth, until the time of the second teeth. Only at this period does the etheric body perfect its own powers in conjunction with the inherited and alien ones. During this time, while the etheric body is freeing itself, the physical body is already independent. The etheric body which is gradually freeing itself, perfects that which it has to give to the physical body. And the final point of this work is the child's own teeth, which come in the place of those he has inherited. They are the densest things embedded in the physical body and therefore at this period appear last.

After this period, the child's own etheric body takes care of its growth alone. Only the latter still remains under the influence of an enveloped astral body. As soon as the astral body becomes free as well, a period is terminated for the etheric body. This termination takes place at the time of puberty. The reproductive organs become independent, because from henceforth the free astral body does not work inwardly, but openly encounters the external world.

As one is not able to let the influences of the outward world affect the child physically before it is born, so those powers (which are the same to him as the impressions of the physical surroundings to the physical body) should not be allowed to affect the etheric body before the time of the second teeth. And the corresponding influences upon the astral body ought only to be brought into play at the time of puberty.

Common phrases, such as, "the harmonious training of all the powers and talents," and the like cannot form the foundation for a true system of education, for this can only be built upon a genuine knowledge of the human being. We do not mean to affirm that the above-mentioned phrases are incorrect, but only that they are as valueless as if one were to say with regard to a machine, that all its parts must be brought into harmonious working order. Only he who approaches it, not with mere phrases, but with a real knowledge of the particular kind of machine, can handle it. This applies also to the art of education, to the knowledge of the principles in a human being and of their individual developments; one must know which part of the human being should be influenced at a certain time of life, and how to bring such influences to bear upon him in a suitable manner. There is indeed no doubt that a really intelligent system of education, such as is outlined in these pages, can make its way but slowly. This is due to the manner of viewing things in our day, wherein the facts of the spiritual world will still be considered for a long time as merely the overflow of a mad fantasy, while common-place and entirely superficial phrases will be regarded as the result of a really practical way of thinking. We shall here proceed to give a free outline of what will be considered by many at the present time a mere mirage of the fancy, but which will in time come to be an accepted fact.

At physical birth, the physical human body is exposed to

the physical environment of the external world, whilst previously it was encircled by the protective body of the mother. That which the forces and fluids of the mother's body did to it previously must now be done by the forces and elements of the outer physical world. Up to the time of the second teething, at the age of seven, the human body has a mission to perform for itself, which is essentially different from the missions of all the other life-epochs. The physical organs must form themselves into certain shapes during this time; then structural proportions must take definite directions and tendencies. Later on growth takes place, but this growth in all future time proceeds on the bases of the shapes which were in process of formation until the time mentioned. If normal shapes have been forming themselves, normal shapes will afterwards grow, and conversely from abnormal bases will proceed abnormal results. One cannot make amends in all the succeeding years for that which, as guardian, one has neglected during the first seven years. As the right environment for the physical human body is provided by Nature, before birth, so after birth it is the duty of the guardian to provide it. Only this correct physical environment influences the child in such a way that his physical organs mould themselves into the normal forms.

There are two magic words which epitomise the relation which is formed between the child and its environment. These are: Imitation and Example. Aristotle, the Greek philosopher, called man the most imitative of animals, and for no other period of life is this more applicable than for the age of childhood up to the time of the second teething. The child imitates whatever takes place in its physical environment, and in the imitation his physical organs mould themselves into the forms which then remain to them. The term physical environment is to be taken in the widest sense imaginable. To it belongs not only that which takes place materially round the child, but everything that is enacted in his surroundings, everything that may be observed by his senses, everything that from all points of physical space can influence his spiritual forces. To it also belong all actions, moral or immoral, sensible or foolish, that the child may see.

It is not by moral texts, nor by rational precepts, but by what is done visibly before the child by the grown-up people around him, that he is influenced in the manner indicated. Instruction produces effects only upon the etheric body, not upon the physical, and up to the age of seven the etheric body is surrounded by a protective etheric shell, just as the physical body until physical birth is surrounded by the body of the mother. That which ought to be developed in this etheric body in the way of ideas, habits, memory, etc., before the age of seven, must develop itself "spontaneously," in the same way as the eyes and ears develop themselves in the womb of the mother without the influence of the external light. It is written in an excellent educational book, Jean Paul's *Levana* or *Pedagogics*, that a world-traveller learns more from his nurse in his early years than in all of his travels put together. This is undoubtedly true, but the child does not learn by instruction, but by imitation. And his physical organs form themselves through the influence of his physical surroundings. A healthy vision is formed when the right colors and conditions of light are brought into the child's environment, and the physical foundations for a healthy moral nature are formed in the brain and in the circulation of the blood, when the child sees moral things in his environment. When the child, up to the age of seven, sees only foolish actions taking place around him, his brain assumes such forms as to make him also, in later life, capable only of foolishness.

As the muscles of the hand grow strong and powerful when they do work suitable for them, so the brain and the other organs of the physical human body will be directed towards the right path, if they receive the right impressions from their environment. An example will best illustrate the point in question. A doll can be made out of an old piece of cloth, by making two corners serve for arms, two for legs and a knot for the head, with the eyes, nose and mouth painted in ink—or a so-called "beautiful" doll can be bought with real hair and painted cheeks, and given to the child. The latter, it is hardly necessary to say, is really horrible, and is calculated to ruin the child's sound aesthetic taste for life. Here the question of education is quite a different one. If the child has the rag-doll to look at, it has to complete out of its own imagination the impression of a human being which the doll is intended to convey. This work of the imagination helps to build up the forms of the brain, so that it opens up as the muscles of the hand expand by doing their natural work. When the child possesses the so-called "beautiful doll," there is nothing further for the brain to do. It becomes, as it were, stunted and dried up, instead of expanding itself. If people could look into the brain after the manner of the occultist and see it building itself up into forms, they would certainly only give their children that kind of plaything which is really able to stimulate the creative powers of the brain. All toys that are only composed of dead mathematical forms have a desolating and deadening effect on the child's formative powers, whilst on the other hand everything that stimulates the perception of something living tends to influence in the right direction. Our materialistic age produces but few good toys—such for instance as that in which two movable pieces of wood are made to represent two smiths facing one another and hammering at some object. Such things may still be bought in the country. Very good also are those picture books in which the figures are made to be pulled by strings, thus enabling the child to transform the dead picture into a representation of action. All this produces an inner activity of the organs, and out of this activity the right form of the organs builds itself up.

Of course these things can only just be indicated here, but in the future occult science will be called upon to point out that which in each particular case is necessary, and this it is able to do. For it is not an empty abstraction, but a body of vital facts quite able to furnish the guiding-lines for practical matters.

One or two further examples will serve as illustrations. According to occult science a so-called nervous excitable child should be treated differently from a lethargic and inactive one, with regard to its surroundings. Everything must be taken into consideration, from the color of the room and the various objects by which the child is generally surrounded, to the color of the clothes in which it is dressed. One may often do the wrong thing, unless willing to be guided by occult science, for a materialistic tendency will in many cases hit on just the opposite of what is right. An excitable child should be clothed and surrounded with red or reddish-yellow colors, whilst for the opposite type of child, blue or bluish-green should be selected. For, in accordance with the color used outwardly is the complementary color produced inwardly. Thus, for instance, green is produced by red; orange-yellow by blue, and of this one may easily be convinced by looking for a time on a spot of a particular color and then quickly directing the eyes to a white surface. This complementary color is produced by the physical organs of the child, and in turn reacts upon the corresponding organic structures necessary to the child. Red in the environment of an excitable child produces inwardly the green complementary picture. The activity thus

23

produced by the sensation of green has a calming effect and the organs take upon themselves the tendency to composure.

One rule must invariably be taken into consideration at this period of life—that the physical body has to create for itself the standard of what is suitable to it. It does this through the corresponding development of desire. Generally speaking it may be said that the healthy physical body desires only what is good for it. And as long as it is a question only of the physical body of the growing child, one ought to notice carefully what it is that is sought by the healthy desires, cravings and pleasures. Joy and pleasure are the powers which draw out the physical forms of the organs, in the best way.

A very great error may be committed in this direction by not placing the child in the suitable physical conditions with regard to its environment. This can especially be the case with regard to the instinct of nourishment. The child can be overfed with things that make him completely lose healthy instincts of nourishment, whilst through correct feeding they can be preserved for him so fully, that he will ask (even to a glass of water) for that which under given circumstances is good for him, and will refuse anything that may be harmful. When occult science is called upon to construct a system of education, it will be able to specify, even to the particular articles of nourishment and table luxuries, all that has here to be considered. For it is a practical teaching, applicable to life, and no mere colorless theory—as indeed one might suppose, from the mistakes of many Theosophists of today.

Among the forces therefore which affect the physical organs by moulding them, must be included an element of joy with and amid the surroundings. Let the guardian be cheerful of countenance, and above all things let there be true and not artificial love—a love that flowing warmly through the physical environment, as it were, incubates, in the true sense of the word, the forms of the physical organs.

When within such an atmosphere of love, the imitation of healthy models is possible, the child is in his right element. Special attention should therefore be given that nothing may happen in the child's environment that he should not imitate. Nothing should be done that would necessitate saying to the child "You must not do that." Of the way in which the child tries to imitate, one may be convinced by observing how it can copy written letters long before it can understand them. It is indeed an advisable thing for the child to copy the written characters first, and then later to learn their meaning. For imitation belongs to the developing stage of the physical body, whilst the mind responds to the etheric body, and this latter ought only to be influenced after the time of the second teeth, when its outer etheric covering is gone. Especially should the learning of speech by means of imitation take place in these years. For *by hearing* the child best learns to speak. All rules and artificial teaching can do no good at all.

In the early years of childhood it is especially important that such means of education as, for instance, songs for children should make as beautiful a rhythmic impression on the senses as possible. The importance lies in the beautiful sound rather than in the sense. The more invigorating the effect which anything can have upon the eye and ear, the better it is. The power of building up the organs which lies in dancing movements when put to a musical rhythm, for example, must not be under-estimated.

With the change of teeth the etheric body throws off its outer covering, and then the time begins in which the training of the etheric body may be carried on from without. One must be clear as to what it is that can influence the etheric body in this way. The transformation and growth of the etheric body signify, respectively, the transformation and development of the affections, the habits, conscience, character, memory and temperament. One is able to influence the etheric body by pictures, by example, by regulated guidance of the imagination. Just as the child, until it has reached the age of seven, ought to be given a physical model which it can imitate, so too, in the environment of the developing child, between the period of the second teeth and that of puberty, everything should be brought into play that possesses an inner sense and value upon which the child may direct his attention. All that conduces to thought, all that works through image and parable, has now its rightful place.

The etheric body develops its power when a well regulated imagination is directed upon that which it can unravel or extract for its guidance from living images and parables, or from such as are addressed to the spirit. It is *concrete* and not *abstract* ideas that can rightly influence the growing body — ideas that are spiritually rather than materially concrete. A spiritual standpoint is the right means of education during these years. It is therefore of paramount importance that the youth at this period has around him in his guardians themselves personalities through whose points of view the desirable intellectual and moral powers may be awakened in him.

As "imitation" and "example" are the magic words for the training of children in their early years, so for the years now in question the corresponding words are "hero-worship" and "authority." Natural and not forced authority must supply the immediate spiritual standpoint, with the help of which the youth forms for himself conscience, habits and inclinations, brings his temperament into regulated paths, and wins his own outlook on this world. The beautiful words of the poet: "Everyone must choose his own hero, in whose steps he may find the way to Olympus," are of special value with regard to this epoch of life.

Veneration and reverence are powers that assist the etheric body to grow in the right way. And he to whom it is impossible, during this period, to look up to anyone with unlimited reverence, will have to suffer on that account for the rest of his life. When this veneration is missing, the vital forces of the etheric body are checked. Picture to yourself the following in its effect on the youthful disposition: a boy of eight years of age is told of a person highly esteemed. All that he hears about him fills him with holy awe. The day draws near on which he is to see this honored person for the first time. A profound reverence overcomes him when he hears the bell-ring at the door, behind which the object of his veneration is to become visible. The beautiful feelings which are produced by such an experience, belong to the lasting acquisitions of life. And *that* man is fortunate, who not only during the happy moments of life, but continuously, is able to look up to his teachers and instructors as to his natural authorities.

To these living authorities, to these embodiments of moral and intellectual power, must be added the authorities perceived of the spirit. The grand examples of history, the tales of model men and women, must fix the conscience and the intellectual tendency—and not abstract moral truths, which can only do their right work, when, at the age of puberty, the astral body is freed from its astral covering.

One ought especially to guide the teaching of history into courses determined by such points of view. Before the time of the second teeth, the stories, fairy tales, etc., which are told to the child, can only have for their aim, joy, recreation, and pleasure.

After this time it will be necessary to use forethought concerning the matter that is to be related, so that pictures of life, such as he can beneficially emulate, may be set before the soul of the young person. It must not be overlooked that bad habits can be ousted by pictures correspondingly repulsive. Warnings against such bad habits and tendencies are at best of little avail, but if one were to let the living picture of a bad man affect the youthful imagination, explaining the result to which the tendency in question leads, one would do much toward its extermination.

One thing to bear always in mind is, that it is not abstract representations that influence the developing etheric body, but living pictures in their spiritual clearness, and, of course, these latter must be applied with the utmost tact, for otherwise the opposite to what is desired will be the result. In the matter of stories it is always a question of the way in which they are told. The verbal narration of a tale can therefore not be successfully replaced by a reading of it.

During the time between the second teeth and puberty, the spiritually pictorial, or, as one might also call it, the symbolical representation, ought to be considered in yet another way. It is necessary that the young person should learn to know the secrets of nature, the laws of life, as far as possible through symbols and not by the means of dry and intellectual ideas. Allegories about the spiritual relation of things ought so to reach the soul that the law and order of existence underlying the allegories is rather perceived and divined, than grasped by the means of intellectual ideas. The saying that "all things transient are only symbols" ought to form an all-important motto for the education during this period. It is very important for a person to receive the secrets of nature in allegories before they appear to his soul in the form of natural laws, etc. An example will make this clear. Supposing one wished to speak to a young person of the immortality of the soul, of its going forth from the body, one might as an instance make the comparison of the butterfly emerging from the chrysalis. As the butterfly comes forth from the chrysalis, so the soul comes forth from the shell of the body after death. No one who has not previously received them by means of some such image, will adequately grasp the right facts in the abstract ideas. For by such a simile one speaks not only to the intellect, but also to the sensations and feelings, to the whole soul. The youth having gone through all this, approaches the matter in quite a different attitude of mind when it is given to him later in intellectual conceptions. Indeed the man who cannot first approach the riddle of existence with this feeling is much to be pitied. It is necessary that the teacher should have similes at his disposal for all natural laws and secrets of the world.

In this matter it is quite clear what an enriching effect occult science must have upon practical life. Any one constructing from a materialistic and intellectual mode of representation, similes for himself and then propounding them to young people, will usually make but little impression upon them. For such a person ought first to puzzle out the similes himself with all his mental capacities. Those similes which one has not first applied for oneself, do not have a convincing effect on those to whom they are imparted. When one talks to somebody in parables, then he is not only influenced by what one says or shows, but there passes a fine spiritual stream from the speaker to the hearer. Unless the speaker himself has an ardent feeling of belief in his similes, he will make no impression on the one to whom

29

he gives them. In order to create a right influence, one must believe in one's similes oneself as if in realities; and that can only be done when one possesses the mystical tendency, and when the similes themselves are born of occult science. The real occultist does not need to worry about the above-mentioned simile of the soul going forth from the body, because for him it is a truth. To him the butterfly evolving from the chrysalis represents the same experience on a lower stage of nature's existence as the going forth of the soul from the body at a higher stage development. He believes in it with all his might, and this belief flows forth as if in invisible streams from the speaker to the listener, and inspires conviction. Direct life-streams then flow forth from teacher to pupil. But for this end it is necessary for the teacher to draw from the full source of occult science; it is necessary that his word and all that goes forth from him, should be clothed with feeling, warmth and glowing emotion from the true occult view of life. For this reveals a magnificent perspective of the whole subject of education. Once the latter allows itself to be enriched from the life source of occult science, it will itself become permeated with a profound vitality. It will give up groping in the dark, so common in this particular domain of thought. All educational methods, all educational sciences, that do not continually receive a supply of fresh sap from such roots, are dried up and dead. For all world-secrets occult science has fitting similes, similes not rising from the mind of man but drawn from the essence of things, having been laid down as a basis by the forces of the world at their creation. Occult science must therefore be the basis for any system of education.

———————————

A power of the soul to which particular attention ought to

be given at this period of development is that of memory. For the cultivation of the memory is connected with the transformation of the etheric body. This has its effect in the fact that precisely during the time between the coming of the second teeth and that of puberty it becomes free, so that this is also the period in which the further development of the memory should be looked after from outside. The memory will be permanently of less value to the person in question than it might have been, if at this period what is necessary to it is neglected. That which has thus been neglected cannot afterwards be retrieved.

An intellectual and materialistic way of thinking is liable to bring about many mistakes in this direction. A system of education arising from this way of thinking is easily prejudiced against that which is acquired merely by the memory. It will not tire at times of directing itself with the greatest ardor against the mere training of the memory, and rather makes use of the most ingenious methods that the young person may not mechanically absorb what he does not really understand. An opinion merely intellectual and materialistic is so easily persuaded that there is no means of penetrating into things except by abstract ideas; it is only with difficulty that thinkers of this kind come to the conclusion that the other subjective powers are at least just as necessary to the comprehension of things, as the intellect itself. It is not merely a figure of speech to say that one can understand just as well with the feelings, the emotions, the mind, as with the intellect. Ideas are only one of the means by which to understand the things of this world, and only to materialists do they appear the only means. There are, of course, many people who do not imagine that they are materialists, but who nevertheless consider an intellectual conception to be the only means of comprehension. Such men profess perhaps to hold an idealistic, perhaps even a spiritual conception of the world and life. But the attitude of their souls toward both is materialistic. For the intellect is, as a matter of fact, the soul's instrument for the comprehension of material things.

And here, concerning the deeper foundations of the understanding, let us quote from that excellent educational book, by Jean Paul already mentioned—a work containing generally golden ideas concerning education and deserving of much more consideration than at present it receives. It is of much more value to the guardian than many of the writings on these lines that enjoy the highest repute. The passage under consideration runs thus:

"Do not be afraid of unintelligibility, even if it be of whole sentences; your look and the manner of your expression, added to the eager desire to understand, elucidates the one half, and with this, and in due time, the other half also. For with children, as with the Chinese and with men of the world, the manner of pronunciation is half the language. Bear in mind, that they understand their language as well as we understand Greek or any other foreign tongue before learning to speak it. Trust to the deciphering of time and to association. A child of five years of age understands indeed the words "yet," "truly," "on the contrary," "of course"; but for a definition of them one must go not to the child, but to the father! The little word "but" reveals a small philosopher. If the eight-year-old child with his growing power of speech is understood by a child of three, why should you then confine your language to his babbling? Always speak several years in advance (for in books genius speaks to us centuries in advance); with the child of a year, speak as if it were two, with the child of two as if it were six, for the difference of growth may diminish in inverse proportion to the years. Generally speaking, all learning is apt to be too much ascribed to the credit of the teacher—therefore the teacher ought to bear in mind that the child possesses half his world, namely, the spiritual (such as his moral and metaphysical ideas), already complete and taught within himself, and that therefore a language composed only of concrete images can never impart spiritual ideas, but can only light them up. The joy and assurance used in speaking to children ought to be given as if the assurance and joy came from themselves. We can learn speech from them, just as we teach them by means of speech; by means of bold and yet correct word-painting, such as for instance I have heard spoken by children of three and four years of age: 'leg-fish' for otter; 'pig-iron' for the fork used in eating bacon; 'the air-mouse' (unquestionably superior to our word 'bat') and so on."

It is true that this passage refers to the understanding (before the intellectual comprehension) as exercised in another sphere than that of which we are now speaking, but for this also, the words of Jean Paul have an important meaning. Just as the child receives into his soul's organism the construction of speech, without making use of the laws of grammatical structure with intellectual comprehension, so too, for the cultivation of his memory, the youth ought to learn things of which he will not until later acquire an actual understanding. That which has been acquired in this period of life, at first in a purely mechanical way, is best put into ideas, afterwards, just as one learns more easily the rules of a language when one can already speak it. All the talk of work learned by rote and not understood is nothing more than a materialistic prejudice. For instance, the youth needs only to acquire by a few examples the most necessary rules of multiplication, for which the fingers are far better suited than an abacus, and then to learn fully, by rote, the multiplication table. If one so proceeds, one takes into account the nature of the growing child. But a mistake may be made with regard to this, if, during the time that the memory is forming itself, too much is demanded of the intellect. The intellect being a power of the soul, and only born at the time of puberty, ought not to receive an outward influence before this period. Until the time of puberty, the youth should assimilate into the memory treasures over which mankind has meditated; later on it is time to permeate with ideas that which has been impressed upon his memory. A man ought therefore not to retain merely what he has understood, but he ought now to understand the things that he knows; that is to say, the things of which he has already taken possession by means of the memory, just as the child does, when learning to speak. This applies to a wider sphere. At first, assimilation of historical events by mere rote, then comprehension of the same by means of ideas. At first, a good impression upon the memory of geographical data, then an understanding of the relationship of each thing with the rest, etc. In certain respects all comprehension through ideas should be done by means of the stored treasures of the memory. The more the youth already knows through the memory before he comes to comprehension, the better it is. It is hardly necessary to explain that all this applies only to the period, of which we are speaking, and not to any later period. If one learns a subject in later life, either by going over it again, or in any other way, the opposite process to that here described might be correct and desirable, although even then a great deal depends upon the particular spiritual nature of the student. But at the time of life of which we have already spoken the spirit must not be parched by being overcrowded with intellectual ideas.

It is also true that teaching by mere sense-objects, if carried too far, is the result of a materialistic view of life. At this age every idea must be spiritualised. One ought not, for instance, to be satisfied with merely producing a sense-impression of a plant, a grain of seed, or a blossom. Everything should seem as an allegory of the spiritual. A grain of seed is, in truth, not merely what it appears to the eye. Invisibly the whole new plant inhabits it, and that such a thing is more than what the sense perceives, must be absolutely realised with the perception, the imagination, and the feelings. The mysterious presence of latent existence must really be felt. Nor can it be objected that such a proceeding would weaken the perception of pure sense; on the contrary, by a persistent adherence to sense perceptions alone, Truth itself would be the loser. For the complete reality of a thing exists in Spirit and in Matter, and accurate observations can be no less carefully carried out if one brings to the study not only the physical senses, but also the spiritual faculties. If people could only perceive, as the Occultist is able to, how both body and soul are spoiled by mere object-teaching, they would not then lay so much stress upon it. Of what value is it from the highest point of view, if young people are shown all kinds of physical experiments in the mineral, vegetable and animal worlds, if with such a study one does not suggest the application of the sense allegory to the feeling of spiritual mystery? Certainly a materialistic mind will not be able to make anything of what has here been said, and of that the Occultist is only too conscious. Yet it is also clear to him that a really practical method of education can never proceed from the materialistic mind. So practical does such a mind imagine itself, and yet so unpractical is it in reality, when it is a matter of considering life vitally. Opposed to the true reality, materialistic opinions seem only fantastic, while to the materialist, the interpretations of occult science must, of necessity, appear equally fantastic. Doubtless, too, there will remain many obstacles which must be overcome before the fundamental teachings of occult science, arising from life

35

itself, will permeate the art of education. But that is to be expected, for at present these truths are strange to many; nevertheless, if they be really the truth, they will incorporate themselves into all culture.

Only through the sure conviction that they are the only educational means by which to work upon young people, can the teacher always find the right way to deal correctly with each individual case. Thus, he must know how the individual powers of the soul —such as thinking, feeling and willing—ought to be treated, and how their development may react upon the etheric body; while this itself, between the period when the second teeth appear and that of puberty, can be perfectly moulded by outside influences.

The foundations for the development of a healthy and powerful will can be laid by the right management, during the first seven years, of those fundamental principles of education which have already been considered. For such a will must have for its support the fully developed form of the physical body. From the period of the second teething it begins to be a matter of making the etheric body, which is now developing, supply those powers to the physical body by which it can solidify its form and make itself firm. That which makes the most vivid impression upon the etheric body also reacts most forcibly upon the strengthening of the physical. And the strongest impulses are evoked in the etheric body through those perceptions and ideas by which a person feels and experiences his own relation to the everlasting Universe, that is to say, through religious experiences. The will, and along with it, the character, of a person will never develop healthily if he cannot experience at this epoch of life, profound religious impulses. The result of the uniform organisation of the will is that the person feels himself to be an organic fragment of the whole world.

If the person does not feel himself to be indissolubly connected with a Supreme Spirit, then must the will and character remain unstable, discordant and unhealthy.

The emotional nature is developed in the right direction by means of the allegories and sense-pictures already described, and especially by all which, whether from history or from other sources, presents to us the figures of persons with character. An absorption in the mysteries and beauties of Nature is also of importance in the upbuilding of the emotional world. And here it is particularly well to consider the culture of the sense of beauty, and the awakening of the feeling for what is artistic. Music should supply that rhythm to the etheric body which then enables it to perceive in everything the rhythm otherwise concealed. A young person will be deprived of much in all his after life, who does not receive at this period the benefit of cultivating the musical sense. To him in whom this sense is altogether lacking, a certain aspect of the Universe must remain hidden. Nor should, however, the other arts be, by any means neglected. The awakening of the sense for architectural form, as also for plastic shape, for line, design and harmony of color—not one of these ought to be omitted in the plan of education. So simply, perhaps, might all this be done, under special circumstances, that the objection that circumstances allow of no development at all in this direction can never be valid. One can do much with the simplest means, if the right sense in this direction prevails in the teacher himself. The joy of life, the love for existence, the strength to work—all these arise for the whole being, out of the cultivation of the sense of beauty and art. And the relations of man to man—how ennobled and how beautiful will they become through this sense! The moral sense, which will, at this period, be developed by pictures of life and by standard authorities, will also gain a certain stability if, through the sense of beauty, the good is recognized as beautiful and the bad as ugly.

Thought in its own shape, as an inner life of distilled ideas, must, at the period in question, be kept in the background. It must develop spontaneously, as it were, uninfluenced from without, while the soul is nourished by means of similes and pictures representing life and the mysteries of nature. Thus, in the midst of the other experiences of the soul between the seventh year and the time of puberty, thought must grow and the faculty for judgment be matured, so that after a successful puberty the person becomes capable of forming his own opinions concerning the matters of life and knowledge, with complete independence. Indeed, the less one works directly upon the critical faculty, and the more one works indirectly through the development of the other spiritual powers, the better will it be for the whole after-life of the person concerned.

Occult science lays down the principles, not only for the spiritual side of education, but also for the purely physical. Thus, to give a characteristic example, let us consider gymnastics and children's games. Just as love and joy must permeate the environment during the first years of childhood, so too the growing etheric body must be taught really to experience from bodily exercise a feeling of its own expansion, of its ever increasing strength. For instance gymnastic exercises ought to be so carried out that with every movement, with every step, the feeling rises in the inner self of the boy or girl: "I feel increasing power within me." And this feeling should manifest itself within as a healthy delight, as a sensation of pleasure. For the devising of gymnastic exercises, in this sense, it is of course necessary to possess more than a merely intellectual knowledge of the human body, anatomically and physiologically. It is necessary to possess a close intuitive and sympathetic knowledge of the relation of joy and comfort to the postures and movements of the human body. The formulator of such exercises ought himself to experience how one movement or posture of the limbs will produce a pleasant and comfortable sensation, but another a loss of strength, and so forth. A belief that gymnastics and bodily exercises can be cultivated in this direction is one that can only be supplied to the educator by occult science, or, above all, by a mind sympathetic to such thought. One does not even require the power of vision in the spiritual worlds, but only the inclination to apply to life what has been given out by occultism. If, especially in such practical departments as this of education, occult knowledge were applied, then all the useless talk of how this knowledge has yet to be proved would straightway cease. For to him who should rightly apply it, this knowledge would itself be a proof through the whole of life by making him healthy and strong. By such means he would perceive, through and through, that it is true in actual practice, and this he would find a better proof than any manner of "logical" and so-called "scientific" reasons. One can best know spiritual truths by their fruits, and not through a pretended proof, however scientific, for such could hardly be anything more than a logical skirmishing.

―――――――――――――――

At puberty the astral body is first born. With the free outward development which follows, all that which is unfolded by the world of externalised perceptions, by one's judgment and the unfettered understanding, will first rush inward upon the soul. It has already been mentioned that these faculties of the soul, hitherto uninfluenced from within, ought to be developed by the right management of educational means, just as unconsciously as the eyes and ears evolve themselves in the womb. But with puberty the time has arrived when the person is ready to form his own judgment concerning the things which he has hitherto learned. No greater injury can be inflicted on any one than by too soon awakening within him his own judgment. One should only judge when one has already stored up the necessary qualifications for judging and comparing. If, before this, one creates one's own independent opinions, then these will have no sure foundations. All one-sidedness in life, all dreary "confessions of faith" which are based upon a few mere scraps of knowledge, and the desire to judge from these human conceptions that have been approved through long ages of time, rest upon just such mistakes in education. Before qualified to think, one must place before oneself, as a warning, what others have thought. There is no sound thinking which has not been preceded by a sound perception of the truth supported by obvious authority. If one wishes to follow out these principles of education, one must not allow people, at too early an age, to fancy themselves able to judge, for in avoiding this, one will leave them the possibility of allowing life to work upon them from every side, and without prejudice. For by one such judgment, which is not founded on the precious basis of spiritual treasures, he who makes it will have placed a stumbling-block in the path of his life. For if one has pronounced a judgment on any subject, one will always be influenced by having done so; one will no longer regard an experience as one might have regarded it, if one had not erected an opinion which is henceforth intertwined with the subject in question. In young people the disposition to learn first and then to judge, should be present. That which the intellect has to say of a certain subject ought only to be said when all the other powers of soul have spoken; before that the intellect ought only to play the part of mediator. It should only serve to lay hold of

40

what is seen and felt, to apprehend it as it there exists, without allowing the unripe judgment to take possession of the matter. Therefore the youth ought to be shielded from all the theories concerning a thing, before the above-mentioned age, and it should be especially emphasized that he should face the experiences of life in order to admit them into his soul. A growing individual can certainly be made acquainted with what people have thought concerning this or that, but one should avoid letting him form opinions which arise from a premature judgment. He should receive opinions with the feelings, without deciding at once for one view or the other, not attaching himself to a party, but thinking, as he listens: "One has said this, and the other that." Before all things a large measure of tact is necessary in the cultivation of this sense by teachers and guardians, but occult knowledge is exactly calculated to supply such tact.

It has only been possible to develop here a few aspects of education in the light of Occultism, but it has only been intended to give a hint as to what problems of civilisation this philosophy will have to solve. Whether it can do so depends on whether the inclination for such a way of thinking henceforth broadens out in ever widening circles. In order that this may take place, two things are necessary: first, that people should abandon their prejudice against Occultism. He who will truly associate himself with it, will soon see that it is not the fantastical trash which so many today imagine it to be. This is not intended as a reproach to such people, for everything which our time offers as a means of education must, at first, engender the view that occultists are fantastics and dreamers. On the surface any other view is hardly possible, for there appears to be the most complete diversity between what is known as Occult Science or Theosophy, and all that the culture of the present day suggests as the principles for a healthy view of life. Only a deeper consideration reveals to us how entirely in opposition the views of the present must remain without these principles of occult science—how, indeed, they themselves call out these very principles and in the long run cannot remain without them. The second thing that is necessary is connected with the sound development of Theosophy itself. Life will only welcome Theosophy, if in theosophical circles the knowledge is made to permeate everywhere that it is important to make these teachings bear fruit in the widest manner for all conditions of life, and not merely to theorize about them. Otherwise people will continue to look upon Theosophy as a kind of religious sectarianism, only fit for some fanatical enthusiasts. But if it performs positive useful spiritual work, then the theosophical movement cannot, in the long run, be refused an intelligent hearing.

FOOTNOTES:

1 *"The Way of Initiation,"* or How to Attain Knowledge of the Higher Worlds," by Rudolph Steiner, Ph.D., with a Foreword by Annie Besant, and some biographical Notes of the author by Edouard Schuré. Second edition, 237 pages, cloth, crown 8vo, 3/10 post free.

"Initiation and its Results." A sequel to "The Way of Initiation." Second edition. 3/9 post free. To be obtained from the Theosophical Publishing Society, 161 New Bond Street, London, W.

2 This distinction is important, for the ideas of the present time with regard to this subject are rather inaccurate. The difference between the vegetable and the creature gifted with the power of sensation is completely lost sight of, because the essential characteristic of sensibility is not clearly defined. When a being (or an object) responds to an exterior impression by showing any effect whatever, it is inaccurate to conclude that this impression has been felt. To bear out this conclusion the impression must be experienced inwardly, that is to say, the outside stimulus must produce a kind of interior reflection. The great progress of natural science, which a true Theosophist must sincerely admire, has thrown our abstract vocabulary into confusion. Some of our biologists are ignorant of the characteristics of sensibility, and thus accredit it to beings who are devoid of it. Sensibility such as is comprehended by those biologists, can, it is true, be attributed to organisms deprived of it. But what is understood by Theosophy as sensibility is a totally different quality.

3 A distinction must be made between the conscious inner life of the astral body and the perception of this life by outward clairvoyant observation. Here this latter perception by a trained clairvoyant is intended.

4 The reader need not object to the technical term "Body of the ego," because there is nothing of gross physical matter meant by it, but occult science being forced to employ the vocabulary of ordinary language, the words applied to

44

Theosophy ought from the outset to be taken in a spiritual sense.

<u>5</u> The terms "Spirit-Self", "Life-Spirit" and "Spirit-Man" need not mystify the reader; they stand for those transmutations of our grosser bodies which are the results of conscious effort and pure aspirations; they form, in other words, the Higher Trinity, called in Eastern terminology: Manas, Buddhi and Atma, respectively. (Trans.)

<u>6</u> Were these affirmations to be wrongly interpreted, the objection might be raised that a child before cutting his second teeth is not deprived of memory, and that before reaching the age of puberty, he possesses the inherent faculties of the astral body. It must not be forgotten that the etheric and astral bodies are in existence from the moment of physical birth, although surrounded by the protecting shell described. It is precisely this envelope, protecting the etheric body, which permits of a remarkably good memory before the cutting of the second teeth. The existence of physical eyes in the embryonic being, concealed in the womb of the mother, is analogous. And in the same way that the physical eyes sheltered from all external influence do not owe their development to the physical sunlight, so also education from without should not intervene before the cutting of the second teeth in the training of the memory. Very much to the contrary, the spontaneous growth of the memory will be noticeable, provided there is food for it within reach, and no attempt be made to train it by means of exterior methods.

This observation applies equally to the qualities belonging to the astral body before puberty. Provision should be made for their training, but bearing in mind that this body is still encompassed by a protecting shell. It is something wholly different to take care of the germs which are in process of development within the astral body before puberty and to expose the freed astral body *after* puberty to what it can assimilate in the outer world, *without* the protecting shell. This distinction is certainly very subtle, but without its careful consideration the whole significance of education cannot be understood.